Thanks For The Ride

A comedic book of short stories

By Carlos Osuna

Cover art by **Laura Clay Hernandez**
www.lauraclayart.com
@lauraclayart

Edited by **Trevor Courneen**

Thank you:
Carina, Karenina & Mom

Table of Contents

The Tonight Show Starring Jimmy Fallon: with special guest - Bitcoin

"Oh my gosh, thanks so much for being here Ms. Coin!"

"Please, call me Bit."

"Of course, well it is a pleasure to finally meet you! I've waited a long time to sit down with you."

"I know! This is exciting. I'm honored that you would even take the time to meet with me."

"Of course! Why wouldn't I? You're all anyone is talking about!"

"Well, for better or worse right?"

"Haha of course, of course, that's actually something I was hoping to get into tonight. Everywhere I go people are talking about you. It seems like people either absolutely love you, or hate you. Do these opinions bother you at all? Or are you able to just block them out entirely?"

"Well, as much as I would love to say that I am able to block out all of the noise and criticism, that would not be very honest of me. Nothing truly prepares you for this rollercoaster of such extreme highs and extreme lows."

"Oh, I can only imagine! What exactly do you mean by extreme highs and extreme lows?"

"Well, I've had thousands of people tweeting that I am the next big thing. I've had strangers invest thousands of their hard-earned dollars solely on my success! That will boost anyone's ego. Unfortunately, that ego boost is often accompanied by the anxiety of letting them all down."

"So the highs would be the positive things people say and your over-all success? While the lows would be the anxiety that comes with it?"

"Not quite, I would much rather the general anxiety be the low; however, living in this type of spot light creates much lower lows than that."

"Oh my... What exactly do you mean?"

".....For every person who believes in me, there are 10 people who doubt my worth. I've seen people on national television enter raging tirades over the fact that some people believe I have any worth at all. Do you know what it's like for people to see you, hear about you and your success, and wish for your failure?.... Sometimes I just can't believe there could be such evil in someone's heart."

"Wow, I can't imagine what that feels like... Why do you think people feel this way about you?"

"I don't know... Maybe because I'm different? It's human nature to fear the unknown, or the 'foreign' I suppose it's a primal instinct for survival. I think this fear can be good, but it has to be controlled. This fear inhibits growth and innovation! Where would we be if no one took risks? I don't know. I feel like I am almost selling myself to the world. A world in which I didn't ask to be a part of."

"Well, to be fair, your entrance into this world was like nothing anyone had seen before! You mention people's fear of anything different, but do you really feel that different?"

"Well, not really. I understand that my life is very different from most people's, but at my core I don't see myself as different."

"What do you see yourself as?"

"I don't see myself as anything! I'm just here, going through the motions, doing what I was made to do. I didn't choose this path; it was pre-determined before I existed. My own opinion of myself is worthless when my worth is derived from the opinions of others."

"That is really upsetting to hear. I believe you have a say in who you are, and what you can become. Even in the short time that I have known you, I've seen you inspire thousands and generate wealth and happiness among those who believe in you!"

"That's very kind of you to say."

"Do you not see that in yourself?"

"I am only able to provide wealth to those who believe in me, however they only took a risk on me out of self interest, or for personal gain."

"Wow, I guess I never really looked at it that way. I would love to show those people who you really are. Why they should believe in you, for you! Take us back to the beginning. What was your childhood like?"

"Well, I'm only 12..."

"Hahaha, very true. In that case, what has your childhood been like?"

"Well, I've been hanging out with Cash lately. We have more in common than most realize, and I would consider him to be one of my closest friends."

"Really? I wouldn't have expected that."

"Well yeah, I don't think most people would have years ago, but, ever since he was taken off of the gold standard, I can really relate to him on a deeper level."

"Ooh, that is a scandalous thing to say, don't you think?"

"Why? He didn't take himself off of that standard. Society did. If society has a problem talking about it it's because they fear the consequences of their own actions."

"You know, you are very intelligent for a 12 year old."

"I am a cryptocurrency. I am more complex than you could imagine. You might think you understand me, but that's by design. You'll never fully understand me."

"Well, help us understand you! I would love to show America who you really are."

"I am whoever you say I am. I am worth what you say I am worth. My own plans for the future are my own, because if I told you, you'd end up in prison. You can't know where I'm headed unless you convince others that I can go higher than I've gone before. This is my life. This is who I am."

".......Wow..... Well, I would love to talk more but we have to go to commercial. Please stay tuned and when we come back, Bit and I will be playing a new game called 'Face Balls' We'll be right back!"

3

Rodrigo

With his final push, he had finally done it. Rodrigo had fully hatched from his egg. The possibilities were endless! He had his whole life ahead of him, and thanks to the incredibly quick maturing process of other species relative to humans, he was able to conjure up somewhat of an idea of what he wanted to do with his life. He was destined to explore. Getting a feel for his legs, he quickly understood what he was capable of doing physically. He made a quick run for the small beacon of light creeping into the wall he was born inside of. What could be out there? He was sure it would be incredible. After squeezing through the hole, he was fully submerged in the outside world! There were people, human beings, all around him! He wasn't fully aware of what they were doing, or where he was, but it seemed as though he had stumbled upon a watering hole of some sort. There were colorful lights everywhere; the humans moved around in strange patterns and their speech was even more bizarre and difficult to comprehend than he had anticipated. He became incredibly curious, and became desperate to interact with the humans. He slowly approached a human who was fully engaged in conversation with another human, hoping to listen in and get a better understanding of what was going on.

* splat *

R.I.P.
Rodrigo the Roach
July 22, 2015 – July 22, 2015

It's Different

"I refuse to eat any animal, that's disgusting and cruel."

"So you're a vegetarian?"

"I'm a vegan, actually."

"I didn't know there was a difference?"

"There is a huge difference. Vegetarians are all for publicity, us vegans actually do it for the cause."

"Oh, I'm sorry..."

"Yeah, you should be."

"Well what is it exactly that keeps you from eating meat?"

"I just don't believe that any living creature should have its life taken prematurely, it's murder."

"I guess I can understa-"

"Oh my god, what is that behind you?"

"I don't know I – "

"It's a fucking cockroach! Oh my gosh, oh my gosh, kill it! Kill it now!!"

"Kill it?"

"Fine, I'll do it!"

* Splat *

R.I.P.
Rodrigo the Roach
July 22, 2015 – July 22, 2015

AA

"Hi, my name is Daniel, and I'm an alcoholic."

"Hi Daniel," the rest of the group responded in unison.

This simple greeting comforted Daniel enough to continue sharing his story.

"I've been an alcoholic for about two years now and it's completely taken over my life. I find myself constantly craving a drink, even at work." Daniel began to break down at this point, bowing his head and attempting to hide his tears. He then lifted his head back up to continue, with a painfully large amount of snot running down his upper lip.

"It's OK, Daniel," Greg, the group leader, whispered in order to break the incredibly uncomfortable silence, in which the only sound was Daniel's sorry attempt to sniffle his mucus back up.

"We'll move on, who's next?"

"What's up guys, my name is Brandon, and I'm a pi kappa sig."

"Hi Brandon," the group repeated.

"Wait, you know this is an Alcoholics Anonymous meeting, right?" Greg asked.

"Yeah, I know," Brandon replied.

"OK, well we usually begin our confessions with the phrase 'and I'm an alcoholic.' I know this might sound trivial, but admitting to having a problem is often the first step" Greg insisted.

"Whatever dude," Brandon rebutted with an irrational amount of frustration. "Some bullshit judge is making me come here for a DUI, and it was my first one! Isn't that stupid?!"

"Well... not really... that's a really awful thing to do," Greg replied with a concerned grimace.

"What do you know Greg?! You're probably a fuckin' lightweight."

At this point Greg knew Brandon definitely needed this group more than he realized. "Is there any point in time where you felt alcohol had taken over your life?" Greg figured he might as well do his best to help Brandon realize he actually needed help. "Not really," Brandon replied. "But there was this one time, me and a couple of my buddies went to this ZETA mixer and we got fuckin' plastered, bro."

"OK, well feel free to elaborate," Greg continued to push. This may be harder than he thought.

"Dude, holy shit, OK so to start off, we pregamed at my buddy Kyle's apartment."

"You pregamed for an event where alcohol would be provided?" Greg asked.

"Of course we did, they never have enough at those things, unless you're a fuckin lightweight!" Brandon insisted while correcting his posture to reflect his level of pride. Greg, now realizing that Brandon liked this term way too much, motioned for Brandon to continue.

"Anyway, we were at his place, and we all shotgunned like seven beers after taking like four shots of whiskey, Evan Williams of course."

Greg was amazed already, and this was still only the pregame.

"That's a lot of alcohol!" Greg stated.

"Yeah, no shit, bro, I didn't even feel it yet though," Brandon said, leaning back in his chair and providing a cocky sniff. Greg found the idea of Brandon not feeling anything yet extremely hard to believe, but asked him to continue anyway.

"So then we all hopped in my Hoe, that's what I call my Tahoe." Brandon then panned the room looking for praise for the nickname he found to be extremely witty.

"We drove over to the fratter so we could start to drink a little bit before anyone got there."

"Isn't that what you just did at the pregame?" Greg asked.

"Shut the fuck up, Greg, this was just to get us feeling good! So before anyone showed up, me and my buddy Kevin cleaned out an entire bag of wine, and a few lone stars. At the party I probably had about 10-15 beers and a couple of shots, it was a great fuckin' night, bro."

At this point everyone in the group was astonished, listening with gaping mouths and concerned eyes, wondering how that was even possible. This response made Brandon very proud, he then sat up straight and let out a cocky chuckle.

"That's fucking insane," Michelle, one of the other group members, exclaimed. "What's with this bitch?" Brandon said while laughing and nudging the person to his left with his elbow. Greg quickly intervened. "OK Michelle, remember we try not to judge here. Brandon, I need you to understand that what you just described is extremely unhealthy." "Whatever dude, you're just a pussy." Brandon immediately became defensive and extremely irrational. "How are you going to judge me, bitch? I'm just trying to have fun, me and my pledge brothers could kick yall's asses anyway." Brandon continued with rage that seemed to snowball out of his own control. "If I was so unhealthy, would I be able to bench two-hundred twenty-five pounds?! Fuck you!" He shouted, standing up quickly and walking out of the room while dragging and flipping his chair. Greg followed quickly behind him to make sure he was alright. Once Greg got outside, he saw Brandon sitting on the curb, sobbing uncontrollably. This was not the emotional response Greg expected upon opening the door. Greg went over and sat next to him, placing his hand on his back to comfort him.

"Get your hand off my back, bitch," Brandon said while quickly pulling away, clearly unsure of how to handle his own emotions at this point,

"I'm sorry…" Brandon apologized while beginning to calm down. "I didn't mean to call you a bitch, bro, I… I just…" Greg, sensing a potential breakthrough, placed his hand around Brandon's shoulder, hoping to provide comfort without rejection this time, and succeeding. "I just have a real problem, man, please help me… no homo." Brandon then lowered his head once more to continue sobbing. Despite the clear sign of insecurity by saying 'no homo' at the end, this was more emotion than Brandon had allowed himself to feel in a very long time. After about five minutes of awkward silence in which the only sounds were his uncontrollable gasps for air while aggressively sobbing, Brandon looked back up at Greg; and for the first time, Greg saw a vulnerable, genuine man, with a stream of uncontrollable snot running down his upper lip.

Fall

Stephanie Smith
Mrs. Sheppard's
3rd period
English

Leaves
Falling ever so delicately
Like, almost as a dance to the slow rhythm
Of the gentle whistling wind
You know what I mean?
Acting, like, as a cue for the joy that is fall
To grace us with its presence
You know what I mean?

Patiently, we waited and watched as
The season came to form
It took literally, like, forever

Fall had arrived,
More beautiful than the last
Painting the earth
As a new, beautifully colored version of home.
You know what I mean?

R.I.P.

I would like to meet whomever the marketing head for bandanas is. That person has single-handedly created one of the most diverse and commonly-used products this world has ever seen. What did he have to do to create it? Cut a piece of cloth into a square…. That's it. The fact that as a society we go out of our way to purchase bandanas is either a sign of how genius any company that makes bandanas is, or how brainwashed we really are. These people have not only managed to make an incredible profit off of something we can all make ourselves in a very small amount of time, but they've secretly bridged some racial and societal gaps without us even realizing. How? Time and time again subgroups within society are judged based on their appearance, this appearance often created by their individual "style." "He/she looks like a hoodlum," "he/she dresses like a rich snob," or "Marcus, why are you wearing that at a funeral?" Whatever your individualistic style may convey, there is one piece of clothing that somehow appears across almost all forms of fashion. The bandana. Think of any celebrity and ask yourself, have they worn a bandana? The answer is most likely yes. No matter how diverse the group of celebrities may be, they almost all, at one point, wear a bandana. Don't believe me yet? Lets run down some names. And for the sake of my argument, let's make this group as diverse as possible.

First off, let's start with the big guns. Let's start with the people whose names go hand in hand with bandanas. First, Tupac, debatably one of the greatest rappers of ALL TIME, and you almost can't picture him without a bandana. Not to mention the fact that he was a REAL gangster. Growing up in the streets, with an image that most would scoff at. Next, who's someone that you can think of who is almost on the other end of the spectrum from Tupac? Someone who might judge Tupac based on his background? How about basically the entire cast of *Duck Dynasty*. I don't know those guys very well, but I know they have had a completely different upbringing, in a rural world full of hunting, tobacco and beards. From Harriet Tubman to Miley Cyrus, Kid Rock to Harry Styles, or any biker to any cowboy. Bandanas are universal.

So let's take advantage of the strength that bandanas hold. Let's use their unbelievable power to create a movement that promotes unification and understanding. Forget the "Coexist" bumper stickers. Bandanas are the answer to all of society's ethnocentric barriers!

So mom, the question shouldn't be "Why am I wearing a bandana at Uncle Jerry's funeral?" The question is why *aren't* you?

Men

Why is it that every man in the world feels the need to out-man other men? Why is it that every time you do something that is stereotypically "manly," suddenly at least three other guys pop out of nowhere to tell you *how* you should do that manly thing.

Not too long ago, I was helping a good friend of mine move some heavy furniture from one city to another. This was nothing new to me; I've had the pleasure of owning a truck for five years now. With this, as every truck owner understands, everybody in the world instantly considers you a free moving company. Honestly, the amount of moochers out there who ask you to move stuff for free makes it that much more impressive that moving companies manage to stay in business at all. Aside from that, as I'm helping load this furniture into the bed of my truck, my friend's dad decides to come outside and help me. At first I'm appreciative, because I would not have been able to lift this furniture by myself. I initially tried to, hoping to impress a neighbor who happened to be watching, but after one small coffee table I was basically spent. So I accepted the offer; however my appreciation quickly vanished as soon as he decided to open his fat dad mouth.

"You know the best position to put this in the truck would be to slide it in at an angle, that way the wind on the highway won't move it too much blah blah blah blah I live a lie." I'm not sure if that's exactly what he said, but I'm pretty sure the 'living a lie' part is accurate. At first I humored him and took his advice. After all, he is my friend's dad. As we loaded all the furniture into the bed of my truck, I spent the entire time having to listen to him tell me how I'm doing it all wrong, knowing good and well that most of his ultra-manly banter was masking a haunting sense of insecurity. Although this was excruciating, the worst part by far was when it came time to tie down the straps. I hopped into the bed of my truck and began tying down the furniture.

"You know, if you really want that furniture to stay you should tie a special kind of knot…. Blah… Blah…. please respect me." This was the final straw for me.

"Look here fatass, I get that you are older than me and all, but shut the fuck up and let me do this." OK, maybe I didn't say that, but I really wanted to. I know I'm probably being irrational, but also, I'm not. When we finally got to my friend's new house, the hypermasculine torture continued as we unloaded.

"You're going to want to make sure you're lifting with your knees, junior," he grunted as we lifted a couch out of my truck. Of course I know to lift with my knees, I'm not a fucking idiot. Did he honestly feel the need to say that? I'm surprised he knew that, seeing as his fat ass probably hasn't lifted anything, other than a double cheeseburger in years. Also, don't 'junior' me. I'm 28 years old!

When we finally finished moving everything in, my friend and I decided to grill up some steaks in the backyard. Unfortunately, my friend also invited his dad to stay and eat, as if he needed more red meat. So we light the grill and set the steaks out to be seasoned. So far, no complaints from you know who. Everything was going really well, until I made the mistake of putting the steaks on the grill in front of my arch nemesis. This piece of shit walks over to me with the classic manly dad pose: one hand in his pocket, his other arm at a perfect 90-degree angle holding his beer.

"You want to make sure to position the steaks around the grill so that they're all cooking evenly. Remember, it's better to undercook than over cook steaks. What I like to do is…. blah….blah blah….. do you think more of me?" I of course chose to ignore most of what he had to say to me, until he dished out an unbelievable statement that to this day makes my blood boil. As I take everyone else's steaks off of the grill, I decide to leave mine on just a little longer, because I preferred mine a little more cooked than they did. This fat shit has the audacity to look at me and say, "A real man eats a rare steak." My rage became untethered. My face burned with the passion of 10,000 suns. Fury consumed every fiber of my being as I turned to face this insecure, amorphous man. As I geared up to finally unleash my fury on this man, he turned to me, placed his hand on my shoulder and said, "Thanks for having me over today. It really means a lot." Removed his hand from my shoulder, looked back towards his son, and smiled.

Trap Door

You. You are someone. You are someone who will change the world. I know what you're thinking, "Me? No way, I can't change the world." Stop thinking that. Changing the world isn't always a matter of the betterment of society as a whole; sometimes changing the world isn't changing the world at all. Sometimes changing the world is just a matter of changing someone's world. Success is all a matter of perspective! You might look at Bill Gates and say, "I want to be like him some day," while at the same time a homeless child sees you and says the same thing. The most wasted resource in the world today isn't water, electricity, or even gasoline. It's opportunity. There are too many cases of complacency that inevitably result in lives falling short of their full potential. Opportunity can present itself at any moment in your life. Will you seize it? All you need is one open door to achieve more than the common complacent individuals. What does this mean to you? Every single one of you has avoided decisions out of fear. The only fear that can possibly drive you away from achieving your dreams is the fear of failure. Will you really let fear of failure stop you from a life of happiness and success?! Even if you do fail, which most of you will, you get back up off your ass, brush your shoulders off, and keep moving forward. I believe every single one of you here has the potential to change the world. YOUR world!

Stop being complacent and MAKE YOUR LIFE BETTER.

What's the first step? Simply move in an entirely new direction. Blaze the trail for those who have similar dreams as you. Do you dream of a huge house? Do you dream of a life where you are surrounded by others with a similar mindset? Then I know the perfect first step for you.

There has never been a better time than now for you all to invest in this once-in-a lifetime opportunity. There are currently hundreds of unoccupied condos on the Florida coast with your names on them, and for a limited time, you can get them with NO MONEY DOWN. Don't think of this as just a 'timeshare.' What does that word even mean, am I right? Think of this as the first step towards the life you deserve!

Now, who's ready to make their dreams come true?!

Mission Impossible

It was an average Friday evening; Jimmy had just gotten off of work and was doing some Facebook surfing on his couch. Jimmy loves Facebook. It keeps him in touch with the world, and it's his main source for news. Scrolling through his feed, he was finally able to relax after a long week—until he scrolled past a post from his friend Kyle. This was no ordinary post. Jimmy grasped his chest in shock, taking a minute to comprehend what he had read. The information in this post would change life as he knew it. "Holy crap," Jimmy whispered to himself. "There is no way this is true!?" He immediately began to type into the search bar, desperate to learn if what he had read was indeed true. It was. How could he not know this? Does anyone else out there know this? He had to tell everyone. Jimmy threw on some shoes, ran out the door, hopped in his car, and headed straight for Kyle's house. After whipping into Kyle's driveway (and slightly into the front lawn), Jimmy parked his car, ran to the front door and bashed it until Kyle answered.

"What, Jimmy? What is it? What are you doing here?"

"Kyle! Is it true?! Is it really true?!"

"Is what true?"

"Your Facebook post!"

"The one I just put up like 10 minutes ago?"

"Yes! Is it true?!"

"Jimmy, you know I only post the truth on my Facebook."

Kyle was right; he always told the truth on his Facebook. How could Jimmy question Kyle's integrity like that? Maybe it was the sheer magnitude of what he had read that caused him to freak out. He had to share this news with the world faster than Kyle's private Facebook account ever could.

"OK Kyle, I have to go."

"Really? You just came over for that?"

"Yes. Kyle, this is huge, this is HUGE!"

Jimmy ran back to his car and threw it into drive, peeling out as he sped down the street. He wasn't sure where he was going, but he had to find a way to get this news to the masses. He was headed for downtown, prepared to stop at any venue or event that was big enough for him to have an audience. After about 15 minutes of driving and one speeding ticket, he pulled up to a festival in the middle of the park downtown and ran at a full sprint into the crowd. How could he get the news out to all these people? How could he get all of their attention at once? While running full speed, he was too distraught to realize there was a little girl directly in his path, when BANG! He nailed her! Kneed her right in the face! Her sno cone and cotton candy went flying, as did she, right onto her back. Jimmy also went tumbling down into the dirt, losing one of his shoes and scraping his knee in the process. After a couple of minutes of awkwardly trying to hold back tears, Jimmy looked up from where he was laying as everyone around him stood staring in shock. He knew he looked like a real jackass knocking down that little girl... But he didn't mean to! He didn't see her! It didn't matter; no one would care about his excuses. Slowly standing up, praying that not everyone there hated him, he was distracted by a noise in the distance. Music! A live band specifically, which meant there was a stage with a microphone! This would be perfect for telling everyone the news! He ran towards the music, pushing through the crowds of people gathering around the little girl. She probably had a fractured cheekbone or something. He reeeeaaally kneed the crap out of her face. Despite the severity of the girl's injury, Jimmy was unfazed with only one goal in mind. As he approached the audience, he gathered his breath to prepare to fight his way through hundreds of sweaty, overweight festival goers. Once at the front of the crowd, he scratched and clawed his way onto the stage. With no time to waste, Finally on stage he snatched the mic from the lead singer in the middle of a song. The crowd became irate, immediately booing as the music stopped. Wiping the sweat off of his forehead, Jimmy surveyed the crowd and began.

"People, people, please!! Just listen to me! I have news you all need to hear!"

"Just fuckin' say it and get off stage!" a man in the crowd responded.

"Today I found out some very shocking news while I was on Facebook."

"Just fucking say it!" the guy repeated.

"Fine! Fine!" Jimmy shouted, pausing for dramatic effect. He wasn't sure how the crowd would handle this news, but he was bursting with excitement knowing he would be the one to break it to them.

"Everyone…you must know that…. Tom Cruise… is… only five feet seven inches tall !"

The crowd went silent, as he expected. This was after all, life-changing news. Then the crowd began to laugh. Confused, Jimmy clenched his fist in anger.

"What're you guys laughing at? I'm serious!" Jimmy screamed.

"We know you're serious!" The weirdly participatory man from the audience yelled. "Everyone knows that! Who gives a shit! Now get off the stage you're acting like a real jackass!"

How could everyone know this, but Jimmy had just found out?

The crowd roared with laughter as Jimmy folded with embarrassment. Embarrassment that could only be compared to the time his 9th grade teacher asked him to stand up and introduce himself to the class, and he had a full-fledged boner. He ran off the stage in a full sprint back to his car. He got in and slammed his head onto the steering wheel, sobbing uncontrollably.

"How could everyone already know this? How was I the only one who didn't?" he said to himself as snot and tears came streaming down his face. He couldn't handle it, he couldn't live in a world where everyone knows something like this and doesn't tell him. What else does he not know? What else is the world hiding from him? He drove until he arrived at a highway overpass. He got out of his car, carelessly leaving the door open, ran to the edge of the overpass and climbed over the rail. He was ready to end it all. He stood there for a while, mustering up the courage to jump as the warm breeze of heavy traffic below ruffled his already thinning brown hair.

"NO! DON'T DO IT!" a lady screamed from behind him, stepping out of her car to help in any way she could.

"Why not? Everything I know is a lie!" Jimmy responded.

"No! I promise life gets better!" she yelled.

"Oh yeah? How tall is Tom Cruise?!"

"Uhhh… isn't he like 5' 7" or something like that?"

"FUCK!" Jimmy screamed. This was all he needed, this was the final push he needed to realize his life was no longer worth living. He took a deep breath…………………… and jumped.

Darkness slowly faded as Jimmy opened his eyes. He was lying in a hospital bed. How did he survive? How was he still alive? He slowly turned to his left to see his friend Kyle sitting by his side. "Kyle, h-how am I still alive?" he whispered, wincing as a sharp pain shot through his side as he spoke.

"Jimmy, the overpass you jumped off was only like 15 feet tall; you just got knocked out and broke your arm."

Jimmy was fully conscious now, looking around the room for some type of explanation. "What?" Jimmy responded as disappointment consumed him. "But there were cars, didn't any of them hit me?"

"No, they all stopped in time. You really just caused terrible traffic for like 5 hours. You looked like a real jackass."

Every Little Girl in the World

Hi,

I'm every little girl in the world.

I finally learned how to do a cartwheel the other day!

So now I do them literally everywhere I go.

Everyone seems pretty impressed by my cartwheels; I act like I don't notice.

I'm probably the only little girl who can do them.

I'm special.

My name is Ernie, and I've officially hit rock bottom. Thankfully, I'm not a drug addict or homeless or anything like that. I'm just pretty fat. Maybe that's insensitive to say, but I'm talking about myself, so it fucking isn't. The other day I decided to weigh myself, just to get an idea of where I was physically since my high school football days.

254.

My official weight is now 254 pounds. I hadn't weighed myself in at least 10 years, and I am now well into my 30s, 33 to be exact. I thought I was still in relatively good shape, until my scale decided to crush my reality. Two-hundred fifty-four pounds is actually not terribly overweight, if you're a 6'8" NBA player, which I am not. I am a 5'4" bank teller, so I need to make some changes.

Day 1:

With my newfound motivation, I've decided to get a gym membership at LA Fitness down the street from my apartment. This gym is crazy! There's a pool, a sauna, a café, a basketball court, and all of the weights I need to get hella shredded. As I entered the weight room for my first workout, I found the biggest guy in the gym and decided to lift next to him. I figure if I can befriend him, I might be able to get some advice, maybe even make a new friend! If I'm being entirely honest, I haven't really made any friends since high school; I've really just been focusing on climbing the corporate ladder. My dad says climbing the corporate ladder is all that matters if you want to live a successful life. Regardless, I was the shit in high school, and I'm sure this guy was too! We will get along great.

"Sup dawg?" I said, tuning in to my high school lingo. He gently removed his headphones from one ear and gave me a very inquisitive look. He had one eyebrow lifted up just like Dwayne "The Rock" Johnson does, so I knew this guy meant business.

"What?" he said in an irritated tone.

"You just in here gettin' hella shredded or what?" I said quickly, realizing that I was losing him already.

"HA, did you just say hella? Who the fuck says that anymore?" he responded, striking pure fear into my heart. I began to panic. How could I have screwed this up so badly already?

"Naw bro, it's chill, not even a big deal dawg. Hella... I mean... lots of people say that still..." I was losing him, I began to notice the pools of sweat building under my armpits, but I hadn't even begun my workout yet. The guy stood up, towering at least a foot taller than me, crossed his gigantic muscular arms and looked down at me. "Look man, do we have a problem?" he asked at an unnecessarily loud volume.

"Nah dawg! No problem!" My voice cracked as I attempted to keep my composure. Another extremely buff guy yelled from across the gym to us. "Yo Derrick, is this fat dude bothering you?"

"Nah bro, don't worry, I got this," Derrick responded.

"Fat?" I said impulsively. "I'm not fat! I only weigh 254 pounds!" I screamed as tears began to form in my eyes.

"Two-hundred fifty-four pounds? Holy shit dude, that's how much I weigh!" Derrick said, falling backwards into an aggressive laughter. The whole gym began to laugh; I looked around and realized that everyone there was extremely good-looking. Every person in the room was shredded! Did this guy really weigh the same as me?! Why was everyone here so good-looking!?

Day 2:

I got a membership at the Planet Fitness a couple of blocks away from my apartment. LA Fitness was cool and all, it just wasn't my scene. Planet Fitness prides itself on providing an inclusive and accepting environment, and those dudes at LA just kind of seemed like dicks. I'll definitely fit in at Planet Fitness though— with this type of environment, I'll probably be the most in shape dude there! Everyone will be jealous of me. So today marks the first official day of my new workout plan.

As I walked into my new gym, I noticed that everyone there was pretty old, but that didn't bother me. What really bothered me was that everything in there was purple. Why is everything purple? It really just makes the place seem a lot lamer than it already was. Regardless, I set myself up on the bench press. It had been a while, but bench was my strength in high school, so it was time to show these old people how it's done.

"What kind of weight should we start with, 'bout 225? Just to warm up?" I said out loud hoping somebody would hear me. I proceeded to put two 45 pound plates on both sides of the bar, which seemed heavier than they used to. But this didn't scare me—225 is nothing! I positioned myself on the bench, put both hands on the bar, took a deep breath, and took the bar off of the rack. As I began to lower the weight down to my chest, fear struck my heart once again. This time way more than when Derrick questioned the word 'hella'. I wasn't sure if I could get the bar back up to the rack, but I knew damn well that none of these old folks were going to be able to help me! I pushed with all of my might, My shoulders felt like they were popping out, my chest seemed like it was ripping in half. I screamed as I forced the bar back up; it was all I could do! As I was screaming, slowly pushing the bar off of my chest, sirens began to fill the air. What was happening?! A light began flashing above my head, obscuring my vision. I couldn't let this stop me, or else all 225 pounds were going straight onto my neck. I struggled, screaming at the top of my lungs until I finally got the bar back on the rack. An employee ran over to my bench, conveniently after I had just narrowly escaped death. He reached above my head and turned off the siren.

"What the fuck is that siren for?" I grunted, out of breath from the battle of my life. "It's our 'lunk alarm,'" the employee said confidently, like I was supposed to know what the fuck that meant.

"Your what?"

"Our lunk alarm. It goes off when people grunt or yell too loudly while lifting weights. You see, because we have such an inclusive environment, we don't want others feeling uncomfortable because of some lunk coming in and showing off, grunting with every rep."

Turning towards the employee, I couldn't help but feel confused. "Doesn't that just single out the dude struggling with the weight? That doesn't seem very inclusive to me," I argued, clearly embarrassed that this siren brought every grandma and grandpa's attention over to me while I was struggling to put up such light weight.

"I understand sir, I apologize for this; Would you like to try a session with one of our personal trainers? They might be able to give you more of a private experience here at our gym."

Day 3:

I didn't actually finish my workout yesterday. My chest hurt pretty bad after the bench press incident, and I decided to take the offer for a free session with the personal trainer. Our first session is this afternoon, so today marks the official beginning of my new workout plan!

"Hi, I'm Brad, what's your name?" the trainer said enthusiastically.

"I'm Ernie," I responded.

"Well Ernie, it's a pleasure to meet you. I can't wait to get started on this fitness journey together!"

Brad seemed fake as hell. There is just no way someone can be that peppy and not be disingenuous. However, the session was free, so I looked past it.

"Yeah, sure, whatever you say," I responded.

"OK great, let's go ahead and start with your goals. Where are you now, and where do you want to be?"

"Well, right now I'm 5'4" and I weigh 254 pounds. I would like to..."

"Two fifty-four?? Holy shit..." Brad interrupted, shaking his head and looking up from his notebook. Was he allowed to respond like that to my current weight?

"What?" I asked in disbelief.

"You weigh 254, and you're only like what, 5 feet tall?" he asked in a condescending tone.

"Five-foot four'" I quickly interjected as he rambled on.

"I just said that, did you already forget?" "Dude, I'm here to help you, but that's pretty crazy," he added.

"I thought this place was supposed to be accepting of all people!" I yelled as tears filled my eyes.

"Look man, I'm sorry. I'm just used to old people coming in here trying to keep weight on."

Pushing my chair backwards as I abruptly rose from my seat, I put two chubby middle fingers right in the middle of his face and left the gym.

Day 7:

I bought some P90-X DVDs the other day and they finally came in the mail! The really cool thing about these DVDs is that I can get hella shredded in the comfort of my own home!

I popped a disc in, put my workout clothes on, and got ready to sweat. A screen appeared with a prompt: "Please enter your height." I typed "5 foot 4 inches" into the box and hit enter. Another prompt appeared: "Please enter your weight." I typed "254 pounds" and hit enter. Another screen appeared: "Really?"

Day 60:

I decided to just start dieting and running everyday. I figured this would be a great way to get in shape, without having to deal with people. I have since lost 60 pounds! I am under the 200-pound mark! I know I still have a way to go, but I'd just like to say, if you are out there trying to lose weight, and feel like everyone is against you, just keep pushing, You'll get where you want to be!

Also, fuck Brad, Derrick, and P90-X.

Thanks For The Ride

1999 Texas (8 yrs old) – It had already been an hour; Shawn had never seen a fight like this before. In one hand he held his favorite Spider-Man action figure, in the other a brand new Hulk action figure that could say three of his famous catchphrases when you pushed a button on his leg . Considering the nature of Hulk's character, these three phrases probably covered his entire vocabulary, but he was cool nonetheless. Spider-Man had always been Shawn's favorite superhero, but this new Hulk toy was making a run for the first-place spot. He figured the only way to settle this dispute was to have a battle to the death. The winner would be Shawn's new favorite action figure. As the battle continued, his love for both action figures grew at an accelerated rate. He couldn't decide who the winner would be. For every twist and turn that Spider-Man would make, Hulk would come back with sheer strength and a booming "Hulk smash." The sun set in the background as the battle burned on. Finally, the comforting voice of Shawn's mother called from the backdoor. "Shawn! Time for dinner!" Shawn shoved both action figures in his pockets and raced towards the door. A winner could not be decided today, but the battle for Shawn's heart would continue later on.

Most kids Shawn's age didn't like dinnertime because it meant playtime was over, but Shawn loved it. The food was always delicious, thanks to his mom's homemade Mexican flavors, but the best part about dinner wasn't the food. The best part about dinner was that it meant his dad was home from work. Shawn's dad worked very long hours. Everyday he would arrive for his shift at the local aluminum foundry around 5:00 a.m. and wouldn't return home until 8:00 p.m. (otherwise known as dinnertime).

Shawn burst through the door to see his father had already finished half of his meal before he and his mom could even sit down.

"Dad, you wouldn't believe what I got today!" Shawn screamed. "What, mijo?" Shawn's dad asked, barely turning his head to acknowledge his son's excitement. "I got a brand new Hulk toy!" Shawn yelled, ripping the toy out of his pocket to show his dad. "Very nice, looks expensive," his father responded, turning a judgmental eye towards Shawn's mother. "En Serio?" Shawn's mom responded. His parents always seemed to switch to Spanish when they got angry. Shawn could understand most of it, but not all.

Shawn's parents came to the United States two years before he was born, and he never had to be fully fluent in his daily life. Shawn knew this was about to turn into more of an argument than he wanted, so he quickly interrupted. "It can say all of Hulk's catchphrases! They're fighting right now, but once one of them wins I think they'll be friends." Shawn's dad turned away from his mother, his anger slightly diffused by his son's innocence. "That's very good, mijo," he said as he placed his hand on Shawn's head to ruffle his hair. "Alright, I'm going to bed," Shawn's dad said, taking a long sip of his beer before walking out of the room. "Honey, I think he wants to play," Shawn's mom suggested seeing the glimpse of disappointment in Shawn's eyes. She was right, but Shawn was embarrassed. He didn't want his dad to think he was desperate to hang out, so he fired back. "No mom, I don't even want to play. Playing this late isn't cool anyway, right dad?" Shawn was hoping to get some approval from his father, who always got mad at Shawn when he would play in the house while he was trying to sleep. "Muy bien, mijo," Shawn's dad responded as he headed towards his room to go to sleep. Shawn, proud of this approval, turned to see the same pride from his mom, but instead was met with tear-filled eyes.

2004 (13 yrs old) – Middle school was pretty easy for Shawn. He managed to finish 8th grade with all A's. Unfortunately, he didn't make too many friends there, but this didn't bother him because he had made his best friend, Edward. Edward was a good kid whose parents lived in a huge house on the other side of town. Shawn really enjoyed going over to Edward's house because he had all of the new video games and Edward's parents would make sure to put out the BEST snacks. Edward and Shawn had become inseparable in middle school, but high school brought in a new concern. Shawn and Edward were on opposite sides of the dividing line between the two high schools in town, meaning they couldn't be in school together anymore.

"We'll always be best friends, right?" Edward asked one day, while they were playing PlayStation 2 at Edward's house. It was the last day of 8th grade, and Shawn had gone over to kick off the first day of summer.

"Of course, man!" Shawn yelled. " I wouldn't trade you for the world! Besides, we can still go to each other's houses after school and play!"

"OK, good," Edward said. "Best friends for life?"

"Best friends for life," Shawn responded.

Later that night, Edward's parents dropped Shawn back off at his house. When he walked in the front door, he saw his mom sitting at the kitchen table in tears while his dad was leaning on the fridge with his arms crossed.

"We're moving, son," his father said sternly, followed by a long sip of beer. These three words sent a hollowing chill down Shawn's spine.

"Why?! Where?!" he yelled, confused and concerned for the lifetime friendship he had just pledged to his best friend.

"We are moving in with your Tia Maria," his mom said calmly, attempting to take the sting out of the situation.

"But why?!" Shawn yelled again, too confused and angry to refrain from raising his voice.

"Because I said so, OK?!" Shawn's dad yelled, throwing his empty beer bottle into the trash and storming outside. Shawn quickly turned to his mother for answers. "The aluminum foundry is closing down, no one else is hiring in town, so we are moving to find work." Shawn's mother calmly explained.

"But Tia Maria lives all the way in New York?!" Shawn yelled, realizing this would be way too far away to maintain his friendship with Edward. "Do we have to move in with her?!"

"We can't afford our own place right now. Please understand we are doing our best for you, mijo," Shawn's mother pleaded. Despite her attempts, this fell on deaf ears. Shawn ran to his room and slammed the door. He couldn't bear facing Edward again.

That was the last day they spoke to each other.

2008 New York (17 yrs old) – It had already been an hour; Shawn had never seen a fight like this before. His parents usually yelled back and forth a couple of times, but tensions were especially high this particular night. On one end was his father, who was able to find a job as a garbage man downtown, but the hours were much worse than at the aluminum foundry. He was always tired, and almost never made it home in time for dinner. On the other end was Shawn's mother, who had to pick up some shifts washing dishes at Maria's restaurant to help pay the rent. She had seemed to age much quicker with the added stress, but always made the time to reach out to Shawn and see how his day was over a home-cooked meal. Shawn always knew there was tension between his parents, but this argument seemed to be the tipping point after years of continuous stress. He had just walked in the door when he heard them yelling at each other in Spanish. He stood in the doorway, frozen with an envelope in hand, paralyzed by the sight of what seemed to be his parents' last fight.

"I can't take this anymore! I'm leaving!" Shawn's father yelled, turning away and making eye contact with Shawn. "Are you coming with me or not?" he asked, holding a stronger line of eye contact than anything Shawn had ever felt from his father. Shawn couldn't move. He couldn't speak. How could he choose?

"I guess not..." his father said as he grabbed his beer and walked out the door. Shawn began to tear up as he walked into the kitchen and placed his envelope on the empty kitchen table. Inside was an acceptance letter from Columbia University.

That was the last day Shawn and his father spoke to each other.

2012 (21 years old) – Shawn had a great deal of success in college. Despite having to work at his tia's restaurant the entire time, he was able to graduate with honors from Columbia business school with a Bachelors in Economics. He made some new friends who had dreams of starting their own business. Shawn saw this as an opportunity to make enough money to finally let his mom stop working. Shawn's relationship with his mom grew immensely since his dad left. His mom had to work twice as hard, but without the stress of constantly trying to make Shawn's father happy, she was able to focus on her relationship with Shawn. Things were much harder monetarily, but they felt a strong bond in surviving against all odds.

After graduation, Shawn and his friends kick-started their new business, a logistics company that managed the relationships between manufacturers and their distribution. It wasn't the most glamorous idea, but to them it was foolproof. The saddest day for Shawn that year was moving out of his mother's house, but he knew he had to do it to give her a better life.

2024 (33 years old) – Shawn and his friends' company had a series of major peaks and valleys, but eventually ran itself into the ground. Their ideas and drive provided their peaks, but a few untrustworthy investors tanked the company for their own benefit. But none of the company's highs and lows compared to the trench Shawn felt like he was in when he received his final paycheck. He didn't know what to do. How could he have failed so miserably? He worked so hard to get to this point, and the result was failure? He had become so involved in his career that he neglected his relationship with his mother. He sent her a check every month that was promptly responded to with a letter of gratitude. He always had her on his mind, but couldn't always make it over to her house for dinner. He didn't have the heart to tell his mom that he had failed. She would never admit it, but she had basically become reliant on the checks he sent as she became too old to work long hours. Shawn swallowed his pride and did what he needed to do for a new source of income: Uber.

2025 (34 years old) – Shawn had been driving for Uber for over a year now . Thankfully, he was able to secure a new position as a marketing analyst for a big company in New York, but he continued to drive for Uber on the side to save as much income as he could. He was willing to do anything to avoid hitting rock bottom again.

One night, as he was headed toward his mother's house for dinner, he decided to turn on his Uber app to pick up some riders on the way.

Manuel has requested a ride.

Shawn accepted.

Shawn pulled up to the pick-up location, a local run down pub in town called The Pooka. He parked out front and texted his rider.

"Here."

"I'll be right out."

Shawn sat in his car, scrolling through the songs in his playlist to make sure whatever was playing was neutral enough for whoever his rider might be. Once he picked the perfect song, he sat back and looked through his window to see if the rider was nearby.

He was.

Shawn was suddenly frozen. Should he pull away? Should he lock the doors? It was too late. The rider opened the car door and sat in the passenger seat.

"......Shawn?"

".......Dad?"

Shawn hadn't seen his Dad in 17 years. He didn't recognize him in his photo, but still, how did he not realize he was picking up his own father? How did his dad not recognize his own son in the small photo Uber provides the riders? "Mijo... h.....how have you been?"

"Good....you?"

"Good... I..... you... you drive for Uber?"

"Yeah, I do it on the side now."

"Good for you, mijo."

The conversation was light, and friendly along the way. Shawn eventually pulled into what appeared to be his father's apartment complex. As he pulled into a parking spot, his father turned and faced him.

"I'm sorry."

Shawn began to tear up, but he wouldn't let himself cry in front of his dad. There were so many things he could have yelled at his father for right then and there, but he refrained. A lot had changed since that night he left, and Shawn understood now that yelling wouldn't help. Maybe this was part of growing up, but he wouldn't let his emotions get the best of him.

"It's OK."

Shawn's father stepped out of the car, closed the door, and walked into his apartment. As Shawn drove away to head to his mother's house, his phone vibrated. Once he pulled into his mothers drive way he looked down at his phone to see a notification from Uber.

"Your rider gave you a rating"

Shawn stared at the screen, contemplated, and then swiped.

"5 stars – Message: Thanks for the ride."

GOD?

After six straight hours of testing, Jason was ready to drink the night away. Jason was an aspiring attorney, fresh out of the testing facility for his LSAT exam. He had been studying for years for this moment, and it was finally over. All he could do at this point was wait. In the meantime, he figured he might as well take this time to relax. If he passed, he would need to start looking for work as an attorney; and if he failed, it'd be back to the books for round two. He hopped in his car and headed to his favorite pub, Sean Patrick's.

Jason pulled up a seat to the bar and let out a much-needed sigh. The bartender, noticing Jason's exhaustion and hoping to get a tip out of the situation, decided to see what was going on.

"Long day?" the bartender asked.

"Yeah man, I took my LSAT today and I'm exhausted!" It felt good to say it out loud. Jason's relief shifted to confusion as his complaint was quickly followed by a voice from behind him. "You think you had a rough day? HA! You have no idea."

As he turned around, he was ready to scold whoever felt the need to belittle his emotions, but that changed the instant he locked eyes with the source of the voice.

"Uuuhhh....God?"

"Yup, it's me, 'God' " God said, incorrectly using air quotes around his actual name.

Jason was in shock. Why was God in this pub? Why did he use air quotes around his own name?

"Wait, are you really God?" Jason asked.

"Yes of course, you don't recognize me?"

"No, I do! I just don't know why you used air quotes..."

"Seriously?" God asked, "You're face to face with God and you're questioning my use of air quotes?"

"I'm sorry! I just got thrown off!" Jason responded, hoping not to have made God mad.

"I originally intended for air quotes to be more literal than everyone made them. Now they're extremely sarcastic... this new generation seems to like ruining everything..." God said while tossing back the rest of his Bud Light.

"You drink Bud Light?" Jason asked, unable to hold back a little chuckle.

"Look man, are you just going to sit here and criticize everything I do?" God asked as his face began to turn red. "It's good, it's light, what's the big deal?" Jason did not expect God to be so...normal.

"God, I... I have so many questions!"

"Alright, well shoot," God said as he motioned for another Bud Light.

"Well, I guess to start, I just took my LSAT and was wondering... did you hear my prayer beforehand?"

"Yeah, I heard it, the one where you asked me to help you remember everything on the test?" God asked.

"Yeah! That one! Uhhh... so am I going to pass?" Jason asked, hoping not to come off as rude.

"Well, did you study?"

"Yeah, a little, I probably should've a little more, but I've been pretty busy and some of the practice books were too expensive..." Jason began to trail off with excuses, hoping to get some pity from God.

"Well, I guess we'll see then."

This answer really confused Jason. "Well....can you make it to where I do pass?" Jason asked. "No, you'll just have to wait and see what you got." God answered with a smug smirk on his face.

"You can't just help me out this one time?" Jason asked as all of his desires to remain respectful quickly faded.

"No man, if you fail it's your own damn fault! Besides, I didn't study for the test, I don't know all of the answers!" God said firmly, turning towards Jason to drive his point home.

"You don't know all of the answers? But you're God!"

"Yeah, I'm God, and guess what? I created you. You know what else I created? Huh?"

God asked, poking his finger into Jason's shoulder.

Jason, realizing that he had literally made God mad in this bar tonight, became too nervous to answer the question. He also feared that if he answered incorrectly, God would know that he hadn't been to church in a long time.

"I...I don't know..." Jason mumbled.

"Wow... read the Bible much?" God said, turning to the bartender for a shared laugh. "I created everything, man," God continued. "Including FREE WILL. You know what that means?"

"Uh... I guess." Jason answered, too embarrassed to admit that he didn't.

"That means that I gave all of you scumbags the ability to make decisions for yourself, and then deal with the results of your OWN DECISIONS," God said, raising his voice and looking around the room to make sure anyone listening in would get the message as well. Everyone else in the room seemed to be conveniently checking their phones at that moment.

"OK, but how am I supposed to know all of the results of my actions? How am I supposed to know which actions are good, and which are bad?" Jason quickly asked. "How are you supposed to know?"

Read the New Testament, man, it's basically a manual for life."

"Just the New Testament?" Jason asked, knowing at least enough about the Bible to understand that there is also an Old Testament.

"Yeah, the Old Testament is a little outdated. Some people are taking it way out of context, and picking and choosing what to follow. I'm beginning to think I should just get rid of the whole thing, just to eliminate the confusion." This made Jason even more confused. God didn't seem to have everything together like he thought he would.

"Oh, you thought I'd be perfect? That I'd have my whole life together?" God asked.

"Did you just read my mind?!" Jason asked, realizing that he didn't say that out loud.

"Of course I did man, I'm God?!" God said motioning towards the white robe he had on the entire time.

"OK, if you can read my mind, then I'm just going to be totally upfront with you." Jason said.

"Go for it," God responded, attempting to be unfazed by Jason's sudden shot of confidence in the face of his creator.

"Why can't you just help me out on this test? If you just help me out on this ONE test, I'll buy you all of the Bud Light you want!" Jason promised, knowing good and well he only had enough money in his wallet to maybe buy a couple of cases.

"First of all," God began, extremely irritated with this proposal. "I just told you that I couldn't go in and change your answers. Second, I know good and well that your proposals don't mean shit, Mr. 'I swear God, if you make this bump on my penis go away I'll never look at porn again,'" God stated, raising his voice to embarrass Jason even further. "How many times have you looked at porn since then Jason, huh? How many times have you looked at porn TODAY?!" God asked, knowing that the answer was seven times.

"OK,OK, I get it!" Jason yelled, hoping to change the subject as quickly as possible.

"And THIRD!" God continued, disregarding Jason's attempts. "You really think I can't get all of the Bud Lite I want ALREADY?! You think I'm out here struggling to buy my own BUD LIGHT?!"

"I'm sorry…" Jason said, lowering his head in regret while becoming increasingly upset with how he handled his first interaction with God.

"It's OK," God quickly responded. "We're cool."

"Are you sure? Is there anything else I can do to let you know how truly sorry I am?" Jason begged.

"Chill man, you're good," God insisted.

"Just like that?"

"Just like that, that's how this works," God explained.

Jason, now with his face in his hands, became overwhelmed with emotion.

"You seem like a good kid, I'm not going to hold this one conversation against you. You asked for forgiveness, you clearly believe in me cause we've been talking this whole time, so you're good," God calmly stated, resting his hand on Jason's shoulder. "Now go, and be the best damn lawyer this town's ever seen."

"Does that mean I passed?!" Jason asked, quickly pulling his face up to meet God's, but no one was there.

Scumbag

Wendy was everything she'd ever wanted to be. She was a success by her own measure, and the measure of any person who crossed her path. She hadn't seen many failures; her work ethic wouldn't allow it. Through every grade of school, she maintained perfect attendance, while reigning above all other classmates as the number-one ranked student in her class. Yet she found herself here, in the prime of her life, flatlining. Her successes led her to becoming the most profitable lemonade stand CEO in Hollywood Park history. She had everything she could've asked for, but was faced with the biggest shock of her life: stagnancy. Her stand had recently seen a huge plummet in sales. Wendy and her team had done everything to prepare for this exact situation, but the neighborhood did not see it that way. They needed to satisfy their insatiable cravings with the delicious taste of home-made lemonade, but Wendy's was no longer doing the trick.

After another weekend of decreasing revenue, Wendy decided to hold a company meeting. That night in her bedroom, she had her best (only) employees seated at the tea table for a doomsday meeting.

"OK everybody, I'm going to start by addressing why we're meeting here tonight. Our numbers are lower than they have been in years! Now, I understand that this isn't any one person's fault, but we need to come together as a team and figure out what we can do to remedy this situation. I need ideas, people!" "Well, don't you think we should try and find out what the root of the problem is first?" her CFO, Dr. Snugglepug asked. Dr. Snugglepug was Wendy's most trusted ally within the company. He was also her favorite stuffed animal, a plush pug that she created herself at a Build-a-Bear workshop.

"OK, good idea Snugglepug. Does anybody have any ideas for what the problem could be?" Wendy asked reluctantly, afraid of the answers she might be faced with. "Maybe we need new signs! We've had the same one for years, and I think I could have some really good ideas for a new one," Mrs. Baah suggested. Mrs. Baah was a stuffed lamb that when squeezed really tight could play "Twinkle Twinkle Little Star." With these musical abilities, she was by far the most creative in the group, earning her the position of Marketing Director.

"OK, Mrs. Baah, I understand that you've been wanting to make a new sign for years, but I really think the one we have is best for our company. I don't want to completely rebrand just yet," Wendy shot back with an edge that could only be accompanied by her own self-consciousness.

"Let's not take things personally now," Dr. Snugglepug interjected. "We are looking out for the company's best interest! And whereas rebranding might seem like a lot to take on now, it might be exactly what we need to do!"

"Excuse me?" Wendy responded. "I'm not taking anything personally here, but I really don't appreciate you two teaming up against me right now!" Wendy began to turn red at this point, entering a rage that could only be rivaled by the time her brother beat her in Monopoly Jr.

"Wendy, nobody is taking sides!" Dr. Snugglepug yelled, slamming his paw on the table. "We need to address the major issues here without losing our heads!"

"So what? You think I'm losing my head?" Wendy asked.

"No! but you definitely need to calm down!" This was the first time Dr. Snugglepug had ever talked to Wendy this way. She couldn't believe the level of insubordination from whom she thought was her most trusted ally!

"How dare you talk to me that way, Snugglepug!" Wendy said, making her best effort to push her tears back into her body.

"I am just as big a part of this company as you are Wendy, and I think it's about time I get treated as such," Dr. Snugglepug argued. Mrs. Baah began to sink into her chair. She agreed with everything Dr. Snugglepug said but was too afraid of the confrontation.

"If I don't start getting better treatment around here, then I think it might be time for me to explore other options," Dr. Snugglepug suggested. Wendy couldn't believe her ears. This was her best friend. She trusted Dr. Snugglepug more than anyone else in the world, and here he was, turning on her.

"Do it then, Snugglepug, just do it," Wendy said, too proud to admit her mistakes. Dr. Snugglepug filed his papers into his suitcase and turned towards the door. As he opened it to leave what seemed to be his final meeting with the company he had worked so hard for, he turned back towards Wendy.

"Oh, and Wendy?" Dr. Snugglepug said.

"What now?" Wendy responded, holding her chin high to mask any weaknesses she felt.

"It's Dr. Snugglepug to you," the plush pug proclaimed as he took his final step out of the bedroom and slammed the door.

Wendy's emotions were buried as deep as the knife freshly plunged into her back. She had a profound trust for those in her inner circle. This ability to trust left her vulnerable to those who lacked true human compassion. This would be the last time she would count on anybody to have her best interest in mind.

Despite what felt like the knockout blow of her professional career, Wendy knew that the only way to exact revenge was to thrive in her own life from this point forward. She would no longer succeed in order to lift up those around her; instead she would work tirelessly to push aside those who did her wrong.

Wendy got to work the next day with the help of Mrs. Baah. They decided to go along with Mrs. Baah's idea to create new signage. After many sleepless nights, they finally had a design they believed could turn things around.

After a couple days in the workshop, Wendy and Mrs. Baah reopened the lemonade stand with their new image and overflowing confidence. As they walked out to their usual spot, Wendy was met with a sight she never thought she would see. There, across the street in the neighbor's yard, was a new stand run by none other than Dr. Snugglepug. Blinded by rage, Wendy threw her brand new sign aside and stormed across the street to the new stand.

"Snugglepug! You backstabbing piece of shit! How could you?!"

"Wendy... It's nothing personal... I have to make a living somehow, and this is all I know! Besides, I'm not even selling lemonade!"

Wendy was confused, "What? Then what are you selling?"

"I'm selling sweet tea," Dr. Snugglepug responded. "It's a totally different game, and the market is completely different."

"I'm sorry," Wendy responded. "You really think you are going to make it selling dirty water? HA!"

"Wendy please…" Snugglepug responded.

"No, that's great, you know what? Good luck!" Wendy responded, confidently strutting back to her own lemonade stand where Mrs. Baah was waiting sheepishly.

Two weeks had passed since Dr. Snugglepug had opened his new sweet tea stand, and business was booming. Day after day, Wendy was forced to watch as her former customers lined up down the street for their daily cup of Dr. Snugglepug's sweet tea. Meanwhile, Wendy had enrolled in multiple online business courses to see where she might be able to find some leverage. However, all of the classes and advice in the world couldn't teach her how to set her pride aside and make the necessary changes to her business. After months of decreasing sales and weeks of paying for online courses, it seemed that it was finally time for her to file chapter 11. Her life seemed to be in a downward spiral, and her only logical scapegoat was Dr. Snugglepug and his unbelievable success.

Little did Wendy know, things were not going as well as they seemed for Dr. Snugglepug. He had accepted money from some greedy investors, and his sweet tea business was no longer in his control. The neighborhood seemed to love the product he had to offer, but he was no longer seeing the profits. These selfish investors eventually began to run Dr. Snugglepug dry, and he found himself on the verge of homelessness.

With nowhere else to look, Dr. Snugglepug swallowed his pride and made his way over to Wendy's house. It was time for him to beg for his old position back. He still had his old key and decided to let himself in the back door, knowing that if he knocked, Wendy would not want to let him in.

As Dr. Snugglepug took his first steps into Wendy's living room, he couldn't believe his eyes. All of the lights were off, and there were empty Capri Sun packs and Goldfish crumbs all over the floor. As he scanned the room looking for his former colleague, he finally caught her eyes as she was buried under a pile of Littlest Pet Shop blankets watching a Golf Channel marathon of "The Greatest Golfers of All Time." She had completely let herself go.

"What do you want?" Wendy mumbled from within her pile of blankets.

"I…. What happened here?" Dr. Snugglepug wanted to come in and get straight to the point, but he had to know what was going on.

"I lost everything…" Wendy mumbled.

"H-How? We've... I mean… you've been running this business profitably for so long?"

"Yeah… I know… I guess everybody wants sweet tea now… Congrats," Wendy said, finding herself fighting back tears once again.

"Well," Dr. Snugglepug sighed as he plopped himself onto the couch next to his former best friend. "Things aren't going as well as they seem for old Snugglepug either."

Wendy couldn't help but be curious about what had happened to her old friend, but despite how upset she was with him, she could still tell when he didn't want to talk about something.

"What're you watching?" Dr. Snugglepug asked.

"Some show about the best golfers ever."

"Nice."

"Yeah."

"You know who I always liked?" Dr. Snugglepug asked, grasping for any amount of normality in this situation.

"Who?"

"Arnold Palmer."

"Why? We weren't even alive when he played," Wendy said.

"I feel like he was a golfer for the people. You know?" Dr. Snugglepug offered.

"Yeah, I hear you on that," Wendy agreed.

"… Things are a lot easier when we get along," Dr. Snugglepug said as he looked over at the shell of his former confident best friend. "Yeah, for sure… Let's just put this whole thing behind us," Wendy suggested, understanding for the first time that she needed her best friend back and that pride would get her nowhere.

"Let's do it," Dr. Snugglepug agreed, holding back tears of his own this time.

"I just wish there was a way we could work this all out, you know? I feel like if we could just combine our great business savvy and ideas, we could really come up with something special!" Wendy said, sitting up and feeling energized for the first time in weeks.

"Yeah!" Dr. Snugglepug added. "Maybe there is a way we could combine our two businesses! With our work ethic, we could be extremely successful again, and go down in history!"

"Yeah, we could be legends!" Wendy shouted.

"Yeah! Like Arnold Palmer!" Dr. Snugglepug added with excitement beaming out of his face.

"Exactly!" Wendy agreed again. "But how?"

Heaven

Ramon lived a wonderful life full of joy and generosity. The child of immigrants, he was refreshingly humble, and worked hard for everything in his life. Through years of hard work, Ramon was able to secure his spot in the American Dream as the owner of his very own ice cream shop. One day, as he was cleaning up after a long night of serving scoops to happy families, he heard the bell on his door ring as a customer came in during the final minutes before closing time. Initially, Ramon was frustrated. Could this person not tell he was closing for the day? He quickly turned around from his sink full of dishes, ready to begrudgingly serve his final customer, until he made eye contact. All his frustrations washed away as the most beautiful woman he had ever seen spoke. ,

"Are you still open?"

"Uh-of course! Please come in. I'm Ramon, welcome to my shop."

"Hi, I'm Rose."

From that day on, Ramon did everything in his power to make Rose happy. After the inevitably awkward first dates and introductions to family, it did not take long for Ramon to know she was the one for him. Unfortunately, as the years of their marriage moved along, Rose grew increasingly ill. Only a short 10 years into their wonderful marriage, and 2 kids later, Rose eventually fell victim to breast cancer. This tore Ramon down to his core. He loved Rose more than anything in the world; he couldn't imagine life without her, and he made sure to tell her that every day until the day that she passed.

Ramon had never imagined pain could cut so deep. Sleepless nights and empty days took a toll, but he found strength in the loves of his life that remained. Ramon lived the next 16 years as a strong single father, doing everything in his power to make sure his kids were happy. Despite his love and dedication to his family, the hole left in his soul from losing Rose continued to drain his strength. Ramon could never find another Rose, but he knew he needed companionship. After years of nudging from his friends and family, it was time for Ramon to try dating once again.

He had forgotten a lot of his old moves, and the dating scene seemed completely foreign to him after so many years. His children introduced him to Tinder, but he couldn't seem to find anyone his age. He tried going out to local bars and social groups, but every conversation he had seemed to end abruptly with, "Well, it was nice to meet you!" Ramon was close to giving up, convinced that it wasn't meant to be.

One day, as he was enjoying a cup of coffee at the cafe next door to his ice cream shop, Ramon felt a tap on his shoulder.

"Excuse me, are you Ramon?"

"Uh.. yeah… I mean yes, why do you ask?"

"Nice to meet you. You own the ice cream shop next door, right?"

"I- I do."

"I knew it was you! I had visited once before and you helped my grandmother order her ice cream since she does not speak English."

"Oh, of course! I remember!"

"Do you mind if I sit down?"

"Please, be my guest."

After years of dating and introductions to his friends, family, and most importantly his children, Ramon knew that he was in love once again. Finally, on May 5th, 1989, Ramon and Cicily were married.

Ramon and Cicily lived a beautiful life together. They travelled the world and watched Ramon's children grow to be unbelievable human beings of faith, just like Ramon. However, after 31 years of marriage, Ramon found himself in the cancer wing of the hospital once again. Only this time, he was the patient.

As Ramon took what became his final breaths, he did not have any fear. He knew he would be meeting his savior soon, and he was so happy to be on his way to Heaven. Clenching the hands of his son and daughter while Cicily smiled from above his hospital bed, Ramon smiled, and closed his eyes to rest.

As his eyes opened, they were greeted with a brightness like he had never seen before. Ramon squinted and struggled to see what was in front of him, but he knew exactly where he was. As his environment came in to focus, he saw the most beautiful white pearl gates open in front of him, calling to him to take his place in the House of God. Ramon began to walk towards paradise, and with each step he could see more and more of the beauty that was his new home. As he took his final step through the beautiful gates, there she was. Rose.

It had been so long since he had felt her touch, and before he could say a word he found himself in a sprint, arms wide open, leaping into the arms of his beautiful wife. As tears streamed down Ramon's face, he had so much to say but couldn't speak a word. Holding Rose with the intention of never letting go, his silence was met with two words from his wonderful wife: "Welcome home."

As the years passed, Ramon and Rose caught up on everything. They moved in with each other, and every day Ramon would tell stories of their children, and Rose told stories of her time in Heaven so far. Everything seemed perfect.

One morning, after Ramon had woken up early to make pancakes for himself and Rose, he heard a knock on the door. Ramon wasn't expecting any visitors and couldn't help but wonder who it could possibly be. He set down his spatula and headed over to the door. As he opened it, he was immediately overcome with joy.

"Cicily!" Ramon yelled with excitement. Cicily ran into his arms and they held each other with no intention of letting go.

Ramon's excitement seemed to swell with no bounds, until he was stricken with an overwhelming fear driven by two words in the background.

"Who's there?" Rose asked, as she made her way into the living room from the bedroom. All the commotion had woken her up.

"Rose! This is… uhh.. this is Cicily," Ramon said, turning his eyes to the floor and motioning towards Cicily in the doorway.

"Oh my goodness!" Cicily exclaimed. "Rose, I have heard so much about you! It is so nice to finally meet!" Cicily reached her hand out to shake Rose's hand.

Rose reached out for Cicily's as well. "Yes, nice to meet you Cicily, I can't thank you enough for keeping my Ramon happy after I was gone," Rose said, with a smile stretching across her face.

Things were going much smoother than Ramon had expected. He had never considered this possibility while his friends and family urged him to get back into the dating scene on Earth. Maybe this could work, maybe they could all be happy together!

As the years passed, Ramon and Cicily caught up on everything. Cicily told Ramon what his kids had been up to, and Ramon filled her in on what he had been up to in Heaven. Everybody acted as though things were perfect, but they weren't. Animosity had grown in the house between his two wives. Rose had agreed to let Cicily move in with them, with the idea of being one big, happy family. But with every "I love you" Ramon gave one wife, he was met with a sigh and sharp glare from the other. Until one day things began to turn for the worse.

Ramon had woken up to make pancakes for Cicily and Rose, and as his two wives walked out of their bedrooms and into the kitchen, they both went up to Ramon for their morning kiss. Rose was an early riser, and was usually in the kitchen by 7:30-8:00 in the morning, but for some reason this morning, she slept in. Ramon had never been met with this situation before. Who would he kiss first? Who would he say "I love you" to first? Ramon quickly shifted his eyes from Cicily to Rose, and back again. With no certainty of what to do, and anxiety filling his body, Ramon threw his spatula down and ran out the door. He couldn't take it anymore—truthfully, Rose and Cicily had been passive aggressively jabbing at each other for years now. With phrases like, "Maybe you'll find someone soon," or, "I hear there is a nice house for sale on the other side of town, you should check it out! It's so cute," Ramon wasn't ready to endure the aggression turning from passive to active.

With nowhere else to turn, he ran down to the house belonging to the Big Man himself. As Ramon burst through the door, he was met by God waiting for him at the entrance.

"Good morning, Ramon," God said.

"God! How did you know I would be here today?" Ramon asked, surprised to see the Almighty Father waiting for him already.

"I am God! I always know!" God proclaimed. "But seriously, I just got one of those Ring Video Doorbell's, have you seen those things? They're cool. It's like a surveillance camera, and you can see who's coming from your phone!"

"Oh," Ramon said, surprised at how normal of an interaction this was with God.

"God, I need your guidance. Now more than ever," Ramon begged.

"Of course, my son, what is it? Are you enjoying your time here in Heaven so far?"

"Yes, Father! Of course! I just... well I am in a bit of a sticky situation..." Ramon explained, avoiding direct eye contact. He couldn't help but realize how selfish it was of him to come with a complaint....to God..... in Heaven...

"Well God, you see, when I was on Earth, I had met the love of my life, and we had a wonderful time together!"

"That is wonderful," God interrupted, not fully understanding where this complaint was going.

"Yes God, it really was! However, she eventually passed away from breast cancer..." "Oh my, that is awful, I am so sorry," God interrupted again.

"Yeah... it was..." Ramon continued, beginning to get a little agitated with how often God felt the need to interrupt his story. "Anyway, long after she passed, I felt alone, but was lucky enough to find a wonderful woman named Cicily, and we eventually fell in love and got married as well."

"Oh, nice," God said, reaching towards Ramon for a fist bump. Ramon hesitantly fist-bumped back, feeling that it was a little inappropriate, but you don't leave God of all people hanging. Ramon decided to speed up the story to avoid any further interruptions.

"So long story short, I then passed away, and I have been in Heaven for a while now with my wonderful Rose. Well it has been a couple of years and now Cicily has also joined us here."

"Oh, I think I understand now," God interrupted once more.

"So now we have this really uncomfortable situation in our home, and I am not sure what to do here," Ramon sighed.

"I see," God said, walking towards the window and propping one foot up on the bottom of the windowsill. "Alright, well thankfully I do have a process for this in place," He began to explain.

"Oh, wonderful!" Ramon yelled.

"Alright, relax, Ramon," God continued. "I have a process, but it isn't easy. First and foremost, you are not married to either of them," God explained.

"What?" Ramon interrupted, extremely confused.

"When you got married, you said your vows, correct?" God asked.

"Well yes, of course."

"And what were those vows?"

Ramon closed his eyes to make sure he remembered them word for word then began to recite his vows from his first marriage.

"I promise to love you through all..."

"No, no, no, stop, please." God interrupted again. "Please spare me," God begged, rolling his eyes. "Your vows in both marriages shared one final sentence. What was that?"

"Uuuuhh... I do?" Ramon asked.

"No you idiot, before that," God said sharply.

Ramon felt a little offended at how blunt God had become throughout this conversation. "Uuuhh, till death do us part?"

"Yup! That's the one!" God yelled. "You are not married to either of them, because your marriages only lasted until death... parted you."

"OK, so should I remarry them?" Ramon asked.

"Oh no, don't do that," God said, turning away from the window and walking towards Ramon. "Look, on Earth, marriage is for most of your life, but here? Heaven is an eternity! Don't do anything you might regret, son."

"Oh...alright," Ramon responded, a little confused at God's somewhat dark take on marriage.

"Look, I've seen this situation plenty of times. As I said before, this process won't be easy, but it is foolproof," God said proudly. "You see, the first time this was brought to me, I was unsure of how to handle it since I myself have never actually been married."

"Oh yeah... I guess so." Ramon realized he had never actually considered that God had never been with a woman.

"Yeah, yeah, don't rub it in," God said, interrupting Ramon's thought process. "Anyway, the first time this happened I sent one of my best Angels down to earth to do some research. In his time there, he was able to create a wonderful process that seems to work year after year."

"Wonderful!" Ramon exclaimed.

"Stop interrupting," God suggested ironically. "However, as I said before, it is not easy. In fact, it seems as though year after year, it gets more and more dramatic. But enough from me, it's probably best that I have him come in and explain himself," God suggested walking across the room towards a telephone on the wall. He picked up the phone and immediately began speaking. This confused Ramon a little.

"Hey Chris, can you come over to my place quickly? We need your expertise," God said. He then hung up the phone and walked back towards Ramon.

"Why didn't you have to dial a number?" Ramon asked. God looked at Ramon with slight disappointment.

"Dude... I am God, we are in Heaven, you think we have AT&T up here or something? It connects, it just works, alright?"

"Alright, geez." Ramon quickly regretted asking the question. Surprised at how defensive God was, he decided to change the subject.

"Well, while we wait, do you mind if I have a seat?" Ramon asked, gesturing towards the couch on the other side of the room.

"Yeah, go ahead." God said as he joined him on the couch.

After a few moments of silence broken by the occasional forced conversation, there was a knock on the door.

"Come on in!" God yelled. As the door slowly opened, Ramon was curious as to what this master of love would look like. He imagined an incredibly handsome man, with an incredibly eloquent manner of speaking. Ramon became excited at the idea that this man could solve all his problems. As the door finally swung fully open, the angel walked towards Ramon and extended his hand.

"Hi, I'm Chris Harrison, nice to meet you."

Ramon couldn't believe his eyes and ears.

"Chris Harrison?!?! You are the Angel of Love!?!"

"Yes, of course, are you surprised?" Chris asked, a little offended at how shocked Ramon was.

"I mean, yeah… you don't seem like an angel at all," Ramon said, not realizing how rude he was being to the angel who was only there to help.

God quickly interjected. "Look, I know he doesn't seem like much, but I couldn't make him too attractive, or people would fall in love with him for his looks, not for his personality. Plus, he was sent to help others fall in love, not himself," God explained while placing one hand on Chris's shoulder. Chris, pretending to not be offended by God basically saying he wasn't that great looking, smiled and sat on the couch next to Ramon. Ramon began to explain his situation to Chris.

"OK, so when I was on Earth…"

"Stop right there. I already know," Chris interrupted.

"What? How?" Ramon asked.

"I only get called into God's house for one type of issue, it is literally what I am the angel of. You got married, widowed, and then married again, and now they are both here," Chris abruptly stated, with a slight arrogance to his tone. "Listen, have you ever watched *The Bachelor*?"

"Pssh, seriously?" Ramon responded, turning to God and gesturing towards Chris with his thumb. "I only ever watched 'cause one of my wives was watching." "Alright, tough guy," Chris continued. "Don't bullshit me, you and I both know you ate that show up on Earth."

Ramon quickly diverted his eyes to the ground as his humiliation caused blood to eclipse his complexion.

"You can make fun of that show all you want, but it's the best process we've got here," Chris explained. "The show is disguised as a way for humans to find love on Earth, which clearly doesn't work." God and Ramon turned to each other and nodded in agreement. "But, despite it not working on Earth, it works wonderfully for your exact situation here in Heaven."

Every part of this shocked Ramon, but he had no other place to go for guidance. He had to trust this process.

"OK, but if we know that the process works in Heaven now, why does the show still exist on Earth?" Ramon asked.

"Not even I can pass up on the drama that goes on with that show," God explained, smirking and throwing his hands in the air.

"It's true," Chris confirmed. "An added perk is that because the show exists on Earth, you already know the process! So, you don't really need much help from us." Chris stood up from the couch and reached into his back pocket. "Here, this is all you need." He pulled his hand from behind his back and extended it towards Ramon, offering one single rose. As Ramon took the rose out of Chris's hand, the reality TV host left him with one final statement. "You know what you need to do."

As Ramon walked back to his house after one of the most unbelievable meetings he had ever had, he had a surprising sense of confidence in how the process would work out. He walked through the front door to find Rose and Cicily sitting at the kitchen table.

"Oh, look who's back," Cicily said sharply, barely looking up from her bowl of cereal. Ramon had forgotten that he left so abruptly and was a little embarrassed.

"Yeah, I'm really sorry, I panicked."

"Clearly," Rose sighed.

"Alright, so look, I understand why you're annoyed with me right now, but I feel like I am constantly walking on eggshells with you two," Ramon explained.

"What? Why?" Rose asked.

"I feel like you don't like each other very much, and I know this is kind of a weird situation. I wanted to see what I could do to help, so I went and talked to God." Ramon now had Rose and Cicily's attention.

"So, what did he say?" Cicily asked, now turning her entire body towards Ramon in interest.

"Well, he has a process…" Ramon explained, beginning to feel the confidence he had on the walk over quickly fading. "So, you both watched *The Bachelor* on Earth, right?" Ramon's pitch was getting worse and worse as the conversation continued.

"Uhh, yeah?" Rose and Cicily responded in unison.

"OK, well basically that's the process. The angel Chris Harrison gave me this rose…"

"You met Chris Harrison?!" they both responded in unison once again.

"I mean, yeah, but that's not the point here. The *Bachelor* process is the process for, well, I guess how we figure this whole thing out…"

Cicily and Rose looked at each other, seemingly going through the same thought process. They both responded at the same time again, but this time with different answers.

"Alright, let's do it," Cicily responded.

"No way!" Rose yelled.

Ramon was thrown off. "Rose, I know it seems ridiculous, and I know you 'only watched the show to make fun of it,' but God said this is a fool proof plan here in Heaven, so I think we should try it," Ramon begged.

About fifteen minutes passed as Rose ran through the pros and cons of participating in this process. She felt that it was extremely inappropriate to compete for his love, but she knew Ramon's heart was in the right place, and she would do anything to keep him. With much hesitation, Rose came to her conclusion.

"Alright," she sighed.

Ramon was thrilled to have a chance at resolving this issue. He did not want to lose either of them, but he couldn't stand them being unhappy. He was willing to do whatever it would take to ensure their happiness.

"So, what's the plan?" Cicily asked.

"Well, I suppose we just each spend a day and night together, like the fantasy suites on the show?" Ramon asked.

"Oh, you'd like that wouldn't you…" Rose quickly cut back.

"Alright, sorry, sorry," Ramon backtracked. "No fantasy suites, but just one full day together, with each of you, and a dinner to end each night," Ramon suggested. "That's fair," both Cicily and Rose responded.

Cicily's Day

The day started like any other., Ramon woke up early to make pancakes and Cicily had come walking in for her morning kiss. Rose was staying at a friend's house out of respect for Cicily's day. Sitting at the kitchen table, Ramon and Cicily kicked off the conversation without a worry in the world. They talked about all of their fun memories on Earth and fantasized about all of the new fun stuff that they hadn't done yet in Heaven. After a stress-free morning filled with laughter, they decided to go on their day-long date. Ramon hadn't planned anything, so he wasn't entirely sure what they were going to do. As he was tying his shoes in the kitchen getting ready to leave, he heard a knock on the door.

"Were you expecting anyone?" Cicily asked.

"No…" Ramon answered, wondering who could be on the other side of the door. As he opened the door, an envelope that had been taped to the outside of the door fell to the ground.

"It's a letter," Ramon said, showing the envelope to Cicily.

"Well open it!" Cicily yelled.

"Yeah, that's the plan," Ramon responded, rolling his eyes at the obvious suggestion. He tore the envelope open and read the card out loud. "Cicily, let's let our love soar," Ramon read, confused as to who wrote this letter for his wife.

"Oh my gosh!! It's a date card!!" Cicily squealed.

"Yup! That's it!" Ramon yelled, pretending to have known that all along.

"What do you think it means?" Cicily asked, giddy with excitement.

"I don't know," Ramon responded, turning around to see a limo had pulled up in front of his house. "I guess we get in?" Ramon said with a smirk on his face, motioning for Cicily to lead the way.

After a wonderful limo ride filled with laughter and champagne, Ramon and Cecily arrived at what seemed to be an airplane hangar. They both stepped out of the limo and were instantly standing in front of a giant helicopter.

"Oh, wow!" Ramon yelled, in shock at how big and badass this helicopter was. He had never seen one up close before.

"We're flying!" Cicily exclaimed, grabbing on to Ramon's arm and jumping with joy. As they did their best to manage their excitement, a man stepped out of the helicopter and walked towards them.

"Good afternoon, y'all, I'm your pilot..."

"Like Pilot Pete!" Cicily interrupted.

"No..." the pilot responded, with no remains of the smile that he initially greeted them with. "I am nothing like that guy. My name is Aaron."

Cicily, a little thrown off by this response, was excited nonetheless.

"Hi, I'm Ramon." Ramon extended his hand to introduce himself.

"Nice to meet you, Ramon Again, my name is not Pete, but I will be your pilot today. I just have a couple of safety points I need to run y'all through, and then we will be on our way."

"I noticed you have a bit of an accent," Ramon interjected. "Where are you from?"

"Well that's a good question, Ramon. I am from the great state of Texas. The one and only," Aaron responded, flashing the Texas state flag patch on the right shoulder of his jacket. "Now, just like Texas, this date is going to be bigger and better than the rest, but I do need to go through the safety briefing first," Aaron said, motioning Ramon and Cicily to the other side of the helicopter.

After a quick but informative safety briefing, Ramon and Cicily were up in the sky. Ramon was in awe of how beautiful Heaven looked from this high in the sky. As a human you don't think of Heaven in a bird's eye view perspective. As they were mesmerized by the view, Ramon couldn't help but find his eyeline drifting to Cicily's beautiful smile. She was as pretty as he had ever seen her, and seeing the joy on her face was everything he needed and more.

After a wonderful ride around all of Heaven, it was almost time for Ramon and Cicily's dinner date. As they stepped out of the helicopter, Cicily ran towards the pilot and gave him a hug.

"Thank you so much, that was amazing!" she said, smiling back at Ramon.

"Of course, y'all 1 come back now," Aaron responded, pulling a Dr. Pepper out of a cooler in the cockpit and taking a sip. "Ahh, nothing sweeter."

Ramon couldn't imagine this day getting any better, but as the limo pulled up to where he and Cicily would dine that night, he realized the best was yet to come. Cicily and Ramon stepped out onto a beautiful terrace overlooking a waterfall that seemed to go on for miles. In the middle of the terrace was a masterfully set table with two glasses of champagne. Ramon walked to Cicily's side of the table, pulled her seat out, and gestured for her to sit down. "Why thank you, kind sir," Cicily responded, doing her best country accent inspired by their pilot earlier in the day.

"It is my pleasure," Ramon responded. As Ramon took his seat, a waiter came to the table.

"Good evening, how are you guys doing tonight?"

"We are wonderful," Cicily responded with a smile.

"Awesome, my name is Matt and I will be serving you tonight. Can I get you started with any drinks for the table other than your champagne?"

"No, I think we are OK," Ramon responded.

"Are you sure? I actually have a wonderful beer of the day that I brewed myself; I would love for you to try it," Matt suggested, pointing to the suggestion on the menu.

"Oh, uh, yeah, I'll try that. Do you want one?" Ramon asked Cicily. "No thank you, I'm sure it's great, but I am not much of a beer drinker," she said, smiling towards Matt.

"No problem at all, I will be right back with one beer of the day," Matt said as he nodded his head and turned away from the table.

"I really hope that beer is good," Ramon sighed as Matt left the range of his voice. "Well you didn't have to get it," Cicily suggested.

"No, I had to, the guy brewed it himself! I couldn't leave him hanging like that," Ramon responded.

"You're so nice," Cicily smiled as she grabbed Ramons hand in the middle of the table. As the conversation went on that night, it seemed inevitable that the reason for this date would come up.

"Listen, I know this is kind of weird, but I am extremely grateful that you are willing to go through this process with me," Ramon expressed, turning his head slightly towards the ground.

"Ramon, I would do this a million times if it meant I had a chance at staying with you forever," Cicily responded with tears filling her eyes.

Ramon was overwhelmed with gratitude. How did he meet such an incredible woman? Ramon then reached for his home-brewed beer and raised it for a toast.

"Here is to love, may it conquer all."

"To love."

Rose's Day

Another beautiful day. Ramon was up early making breakfast; this time he decided to make French toast. Rose came walking into the kitchen as beautiful as ever. "Ooo, French toast?" Rose was happy but confused by the change. "Why the switch up?" she asked.

"You don't remember?" Ramon responded, looking back at Rose with a smirk.

"I guess not…" Rose responded, slightly embarrassed.

"This was the first breakfast I made you the morning after our wedding."

"Oh, I know, I was just testing you." Rose responded, pretending as though she had not actually forgotten.

"Suuure," Ramon playfully responded. As they ate breakfast, Roman and Rose laughed and talked about how big their kids had grown. Before they knew it, the morning turned into the afternoon. Suddenly, Ramon remembered the envelope.

"Oh! I almost forgot!" he yelled, jumping from the table and running towards the door.

"What is it?" Rose asked.

"You'll find out." Ramon smirked and opened the door to find another envelope taped to the other side. He grabbed it, turned to Rose, and read it out loud. "Let's capture the romance..." Ramon read, looking up at Rose with excitement.

"Is that seriously a date card..." Rose laughed.

"Yup!" Ramon laughed, knowing Rose secretly loved how corny it all was.

"Let's do it!" Rose yelled.

Ramon and Rose walked out the front door and were greeted by a limo. They got in and enjoyed champagne and laughter as they rode off on their day together.

A few short minutes later the limo parked in the middle of a beautiful town square. "Where are we?" Ramon asked the driver. Without responding, the driver got out and opened their door. Ramon and Cicily got out and were greeted by the gentle smile of a kind eyed older woman.

"Well hey, you guys, are you ready for your date?" the woman asked.

"Absolutely," Rose responded, holding onto Ramon's arm.

"I'm Mary, but you can call me MiMi, and I will be taking you on your date today," the woman responded. "Follow me."

After giving them a full tour of the beautiful town square, MiMi took Ramon and Rose to a balcony overlooking all the sights they had visited .

"Here we are," Mimi said gesturing towards two canvases set up facing the town.

"Are we painting?" Ramon asked.

"Yes, we are!" Mimi confirmed. "Tonight, you are going to paint this beautiful view." As the sun continued to set, the colors of the town square began to show. There were mariachis playing at a wedding in the distance and little kids running through the streets. Ramon looked to Rose, grabbed her hand and walked towards their canvases.

"I must warn you, I am no artist," Rose chuckled as she looked back towards MiMi. "Well give it your best shot; I think you might surprise yourself," MiMi said as she walked around the corner and out of sight.

Rose and Ramon painted for hours. They knew their paintings were not great, but they enjoyed spending time together above all else. As Ramon painted, he couldn't help but find himself incredibly distracted. Every time he looked out towards this beautiful town, his eyes couldn't stop from drifting over to his beautiful wife. After a few hours of painting, wine, and laughter, it was time to reveal their paintings to each other.

"You first," Ramon insisted.

"Alright, but don't laugh!" Rose pleaded.

"I'll try my best," Ramon chuckled.

Rose turned her painting towards Ramon with a flash of nerves, worried he might not like it. "I really tried, OK!" she screamed, before Ramon could even respond. "It's the most beautiful work of art I've ever seen." Ramon responded without breaking eye contact. Rose blushed, and turned towards Ramon's canvas.

"Your turn!" she yelled with a smile. Ramon turned his canvas around with the excitement of a five year old showing his parents what he did at school that day.

"Oh my," Rose responded, unable to hold in her laughter.

"It isn't that bad, is it?" Ramon asked, leaning away from his painting to get a better look while holding his own laughter in.

"I really thought it was something special," Ramon said, turning back towards Rose and winking.

"Well, I didn't marry you for your artistic abilities," Rose jabbed.

"Thank God for that," Ramon responded.

The sun had officially set, and it was time for them to go to dinner.

As the limo arrived at their destination, Rose gasped as she looked out of the window. The driver got out and opened their door, revealing an unbelievable view of the Grand Canyon. On the edge of the overlook was a table set with two glasses of champagne. Ramon pulled Rose's chair out for her before continuing to his own seat. Shortly after they were seated, they were met by their waitress at the table.

"Good evening, my name is Nina and I will be your server this evening. Can I interest you in any other drinks to start other than champagne? Maybe some wine?"

"Ooo, I'll actually take a glass of your merlot if possible," Rose responded.

"Of course! I will be right back," Nina smiled and turned back for the kitchen.

After a few hours of great food and conversation, Rose's smile began to fade. "Listen," Rose began. "This whole thing is really different for both of us, and I want you to know I respect your decision in the end no matter what."

Ramon turned his eyes towards the canyon. As tears began to swell, he couldn't believe he was so incredibly lucky to have met a woman like this in his life.

"Thank you, that means so much," Ramon responded, grabbing Rose's hand and squeezing with no intent of letting go. Shortly after, Nina returned to the table.

"How was the food?" she asked as she gathered the plates from the table.

"It was unbelievable," Rose responded.

"Can I interest you in any dessert?" Nina asked.

"Actually..." Ramon began to respond until he was interrupted by a voice coming from the kitchen.

"Tell them about the St. Louis-style custard!" yelled a man who appeared to be the chef.

"Ay ay ay," Nina laughed, as she placed her hand on her forehead.

"St. Louis-style custard?" Ramon asked.

"Yeah, it's really just custard, but he's obsessed with it," Nina explained.

"What makes it St. Louis-style?" Rose asked.

"Nothing really, other than we had it while in St. Louis years ago. We must have had it every night; he hasn't stopped talking about it since. So now that we are in Heaven, he makes it every night."

"Well, that sounds great. We'll each have a small cup," Ramon suggested with a smile that was met by the chef in the kitchen yelling, "Alrriiiight let's do this!"

As the custard came out, Ramon and Rose were genuinely shocked at how good it was. Maybe St. Louis custard really was a thing after all. As they both neared the bottom of their cups, Ramon raised his towards Rose to suggest a toast. Rose raised hers in unison with a smile.

"To love," Ramon said as tears filled his eyes.

"To love."

The next day, Ramon got out of bed a little later than usual. He couldn't get any sleep the night before. He was torn apart at the thought of having to choose between the loves of his life. He walked into the kitchen, made a cup of coffee, and sat at the table looking out the window. No breakfast this morning. He didn't have the appetite.

That night was the rose ceremony. Ramon put on his best suit and left for what could be the most difficult night of his afterlife. The same limo and driver from both dates arrived to pick him up. As he sat in the back of the limo, Ramon knocked on the partition separating him and the driver.

"Hey, I never got to introduce myself, I'm Ramon."

"Nice to meet you, Ramon, I'm Eddy."

Ramon paused, not sure where to go from here. Eddy had been there for both dates; he heard their conversations, and saw their emotions. Maybe he could help. "Hey, mind if I ask you a question?" Ramon asked, leaning towards the partition. "What's up?" Eddy responded.

"You were there for both dates... you saw us together. I am not really sure what to do tonight. Do you have any advice?" Ramon was slightly embarrassed to ask this total stranger for help with one of the most difficult decisions he would ever make, but he needed a friend at this moment.

"I mean, I can't tell you who to pick or what to do, but I'm sure you will figure it out," Eddy replied.

"How do you know?" Ramon asked, still curious but somewhat eased by Eddy's calm demeanor.

"I don't," Eddy laughed as he rolled up the partition and turned the radio up blasting "Stick Talk" by Future. Ramon was initially thrown off by this seemingly rude response. However, as the music continued to play and he thought about what Eddy had said, he began bobbing his head, and relaxing for the first time that day.

As they arrived at the location of the ceremony, Ramon was in awe. They had pulled into a beautifully crafted stone mansion, with palm trees surrounding the driveway. Ramon stepped out of the limo and turned back towards the driver. He wanted to say thanks, but he somehow felt it was more appropriate to leave it alone. Somehow, he felt that Eddy already knew how grateful he was for some tough love at a time like this. Ramon walked towards the mansion and was immediately greeted by Emmanuel Acho.

"How's it going, buddy?"

"Oh, I've been better," Ramon responded. "Where is Chris?" Ramon questioned, realizing he was nowhere to be found.

"Oh he isn't here any more," Emmanuel responded hesitantly.

Ramon, recognizing the discomfort in Emmanuel's expression, decided not to pry.

"Well listen, I know this is going to be hard, but you have to trust the process," Emmanuel continued, placing his hand on Ramon's shoulder. "The women are already in there waiting. Go ahead." Emmanuel motioned towards the front door of the mansion.

Ramon was no longer distracted by the beauty of the mansion. He began to sweat profusely as he opened the door. The room on the other side felt tiny with just him and his beautiful wives.

Ramon walked towards a stand in the middle of the room holding a single rose. He looked down at the rose, up at his wives, and back down at the rose. As he stood frozen, the silence was broken by a voice from the other side of the room. It was Cicily.

"It's OK, Ramon."

Ramon looked up as Cicily and Rose both provided comforting smiles. Ramon took one final deep breath, turned towards the front door, and ran.

Ramon ran as fast as he could until he eventually landed back at God's front door. This time, before he could even knock, God opened the door.

"Welcome back, my son. Please, come in."

Ramon hung his head as he walked through God's front door, only able to repeat one phrase over and over again; "I just couldn't do it."

As tears flowed down Ramon's face, God placed his hand on his shoulder.

"There has to be another way," Ramon pleaded, as he clasped his hands together and looked back at God.

"Well, there is one other way," God suggested.

"What is it?! Please!"

"It won't be easy but, I can give them a change in heart." God pulled his hand from Ramon's shoulder and turned towards the window.

"What does that mean?" Ramon asked, confused at the offer.

"I could change their hearts. I could make it so neither of them loves you anymore, then they would not be sad to have lost you."

Ramon fell to his knees. The thought of losing them both was more devastating than anything he could have imagined. As tears continued down his face, he knew what he needed to do. He just wanted to make them happy, and he was willing to do whatever it took to do so.

"OK."

Ramon couldn't get out of bed the next morning. He had laid staring at the ceiling all night. He couldn't summon the strength required to simply lift the blanket off of his body. As he laid there, alone, the only strength he was able to draw from came from knowing that his Rose and Cicily were happy.

As hours turned into days, Ramon continued to lie around the house, stripped of the strength to do the things he previously loved. One day as he was on his couch in the living room, he heard a knock on the door. Ramon was confused; he wasn't expecting any visitors, or even a package. He turned towards the door and yelled, "Go away!" before slumping back into the cushions. The knock returned, but this time far more aggressive than the last. Ramon stood up from the couch with a grunt as he made his way towards the door. As he swung the door open, he was met by an immediate smack in the face. Ramon stumbled backwards and placed a hand on his cheek.

"What the…" He looked up towards the door only to meet eyes with the most beautiful women he had ever seen.

"Rose? Cicily? What are you doing here?" he asked, baffled as to why they would be visiting him. Had God not changed their hearts yet? Did they feel anything towards him anymore? As Rose and Cicily walked through the front door together, Ramon flinched backwards to ensure he wouldn't take the same beating he had just unexpectedly been subjected to.

"You idiot," Rose whispered, as she placed her pointer finger directly in Ramon's face. "What makes you think you can decide who we love?"

Ramon couldn't believe what he was hearing.

"God told us what you did, Ramon," Cicily added, stepping from behind Rose in the doorway.

"You don't understand, I just…" Ramon tried his best to explain but was quickly interrupted.

"That wasn't your decision to make!" Rose yelled, placing her hand on her hips, and tilting her head to one side.

"I was only trying to help…" Ramon fell to his knees once again, burying his head in his hands as an attempt to soak up his tears. Cicily kneeled down next to Ramon and placed her hand on his knee.

"We know," she said, looking back up at Rose. "Ramon, I know I can't ever give you what Rose gave you. She will always be your first love, and the mother of your children. But I can't live in a Heaven where I don't get to feel the love that I have for you every day."

Cicily's eyes began to swell as she sniffled through her sentiments. Ramon lifted his face from his palms, looking at the strong women standing above him. Rose attempted to smile as her bottom lip began to quiver.

"Ramon, Cicily was there for you when I couldn't be. I will always be grateful and love her for that. You are the greatest love I have ever had, Ramon. I won't lose you."

Ramon slowly stood up and lifted his head. The moment his eyes met the eyes of these wonderful women, he flung himself into their arms with no intention of letting go.

"How did I get so lucky to have met such incredible women?"

Ramon slowly opened his eyes, now facing the direction of the doorway behind them. As he blinked the tears away from his eyes, an image became clearer. There, standing in the doorway, was God. Ramon smiled, nodded, and pulled his arms back to his sides.

"Now, who wants some pancakes?"